dedicated to mom
we love you

a book of twilight colors

Contents

Black-magenta

Some of us
are mixed in the
portrait of memories.

Ultra-Violet Queens
paint Dark hearted enemies.

But she wishes to paint
of warmer times.

Picture your dark heart Love
rollin' with
mine.

Purple Skys

Picture me rollin'
out in the Regal

lookin for purple skies
or maybe an eagle.

there's too much spaces between us
because of the dark seats

look at the skies son
its purples but I see pinks.

no its black
purple fades in time.

but really purple like dads,
And blacks like mine,

black Queens of Hearts,
but I see pinks.
....

nd my father,
a soldier in the war
of memories
fought,
more battles won
than battles forgot.

Black queen of hearts
a straight flush.

nd dad would say
you gotta have heart kid,

we can't forget Charlie.

Yellow

Maybe i'll paint you something
pretty in Yellow.

My colors are NEVER perfect.
But your colors are.

Light shades of Yellow
Yellow my life.

Love and madness,
yellows my canvas.

Yellow.

Flourescent Pink

Flourescent pink is neon
and out shines the most

color me in pink
like butter on toast.

if you'll be the Princess
then i'll be the toad.

And well mario kart forever
down star road.

Perfect yellow

My colors are never perfect.
But your colors are

Perfect Yellow.

Blue-violet

bill murrays
portraited painted in blue violet

I love this color
my favorite color
for awhile

i always forget to buy it
I wish I had more color.

heres a tip
add more color

reminds me of blue berries
we find
that always stain our teeth.

how blue are you>
I tellem im blue-violet
they say
thats pretty.
and I agree.

Red-velvet

Red rover Red rover
send (insert your name) right over...

they never remember my name...
but watch!

when I become famous they will!
 or will they not?

but its ok
because I have beautiful

Red-Velvet socks!
And this is the the color
I chose

So I say...stay warm!
my red-velvet toes!

Sepia Serpent

Photographs of a dog
memories of smog

an eternal dragons
buried treasures
guarded in fog.

Special memories
painted

under a serpents eye

Your works of art
 never die.

October-Black

Smoke black like
mortal combat

my favorite color
is October.

Greys and blacks
For Halloween
on Christmas.

Challenge me?
ill challenge back,

Jack.

Orange

One-two,
Orange is coming for you...

Three-four,
better paint the floors...

Five-six,
get your markers fixed...

Seven-eight,
keep your pencils straight...

Nine-ten,
here's Orange again

one two,
Orange is coming for you...

Ultra-Violet

It's night-time at the COn.
Flouro sound cooler in Neon lights.
Ultra Violet alley is where I roam.
look'in for a find.

LINK-GREEN

No sword-or-shovel in your game.

Links a cruel
green start

show'em
you can make it

through the dungeon
ona
quarter heart.

Twilight

Flourescent galaxies of
Twilight colors
that glow and fade
that pop and glow

Twilight sparkles
the night when "I" paint.

Glitter falls from the sky
onto my nights canvas

invisible my colors are too bright
to see through the Twilight.

paint me one
or paint me none

paint on painter
my Twilight eyes are for you,
painted with clear glazes of colors
forgotten by others
forget-me-never

ill return once more
in the Twilight
I'll float to a galaxy far far away...

...and return a penny wiser.

one for your troubles
and two for ours.

I love you so damn much,
my colors bleed for you in the Twilight

how I just want to see
your pretty colors again.

lovely is the Twilight night
but remember the Twilight
never visits twice.

chaos eyes seen,
through my Twilight dust

ashes blaze in the sparks
that never rust.
Twilight.

SCAR BLUE

scars of blue
lost in the jungle
scars of blue
never let you go

scars of blue
livin no worries :)

scar blue fade in time

paint me in pastels
so I can nevr see my scars.

some color

livin no worries for the rest of my day!
livin no worries
with or without
my scars

!Hakuna matata!

Surfer-silver

Glistening in chrome
flying high
across the stars like some
roman God.

my board in hand.
is all I need.
I am the one who rides at night.
lights all off in the streets
but mine are on

tricks no one will see.
these are the ones that
count.
shine like Silver-Surfer in the night.

Purple Purple

Purple skeleton keys
and boney Jacks claw
brewed with cats paw.

Purple Purple moons
purple clowns-n-haunted house rooms.

Halloween Paintings on porches and window
sills
remind me of Chicago nights still.

Purple Pumpkins
Purple ghosts,

Neon-violets,
in haunted hosts.

Purple demons
Purple nights
Purple Purple sights.

DIEGO ANTONIO GONZALEZ JR

Night Bright Red

Bright Red looks orange
paint brushed on thick makes it warm.

dont ask me why
I squeezed straight from the tube
until the reds die.

I cleaned paint brushes all night.
but its worth it
to make it glow

night bright.

New BLACK

New black dressed down in grey
muted to dull
today.

Tangerine

Tangled in Pearl Tangerine
down shimmering
glittering seams,

i made that you see

they say nothing
looks good
in tangerine.

but I do.

Turtle-green

A shogun
turtle
tinted in Green.

A master of a color
few have ever seen.

Peach

2 players
Peach
and Toad'
speeding down star road...

pastel pinks
we just call it peach.

Cruisin'
in the drivers seat.

Spaced-out grey

Behind the stars of black
 lies a pale spaced-out grey.

Matt or glossy
colors all scuff away.

a perfect color in my
 rattle can new,

but when I paint in greys
I always paint you.

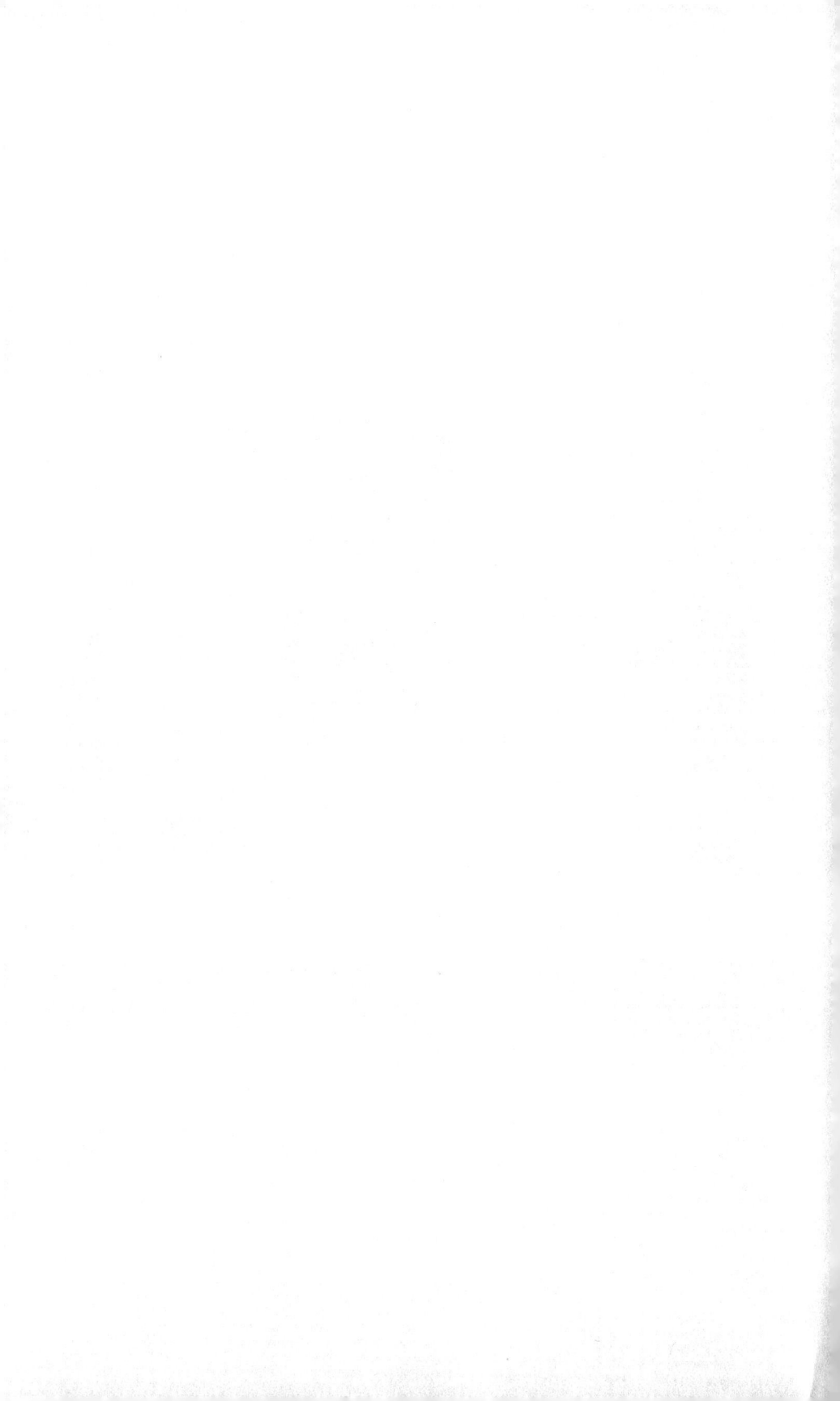

www.ingramcontent.com/pod-product-compliance
Lightning Source LLC
Chambersburg PA
CBHW030559220526
45463CB00007B/3121